HUMAN MIGRATION

Investigate the Global Journey of Humankind

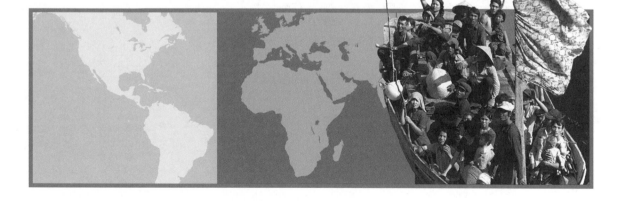

INQUIRE AND INVESTIGATE

Judy Dodge Cummings
Illustrated by Tom Casteel

Nomad Press
A division of Nomad Communications
10 9 8 7 6 5 4 3 2 1

This book was manufactured by Marquis Book Printing,
Montmagny, Québec, Canada
July 2016, Job #121612
ISBN Softcover: 978-1-61930-375-1
ISBN Hardcover: 978-1-61930-371-3

Educational Consultant, Marla Conn

Questions regarding the ordering of this book should be addressed to
Nomad Press
2456 Christian St.
White River Junction, VT 05001
www.nomadpress.net

Printed in Canada.

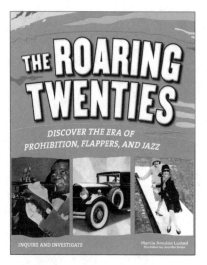

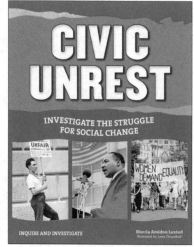

Social Studies titles in the
Inquire and Investigate series

Check out more titles at www.nomadpress.net

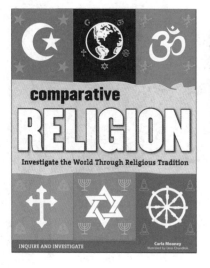

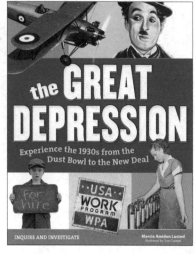

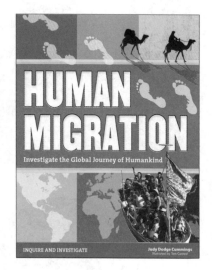

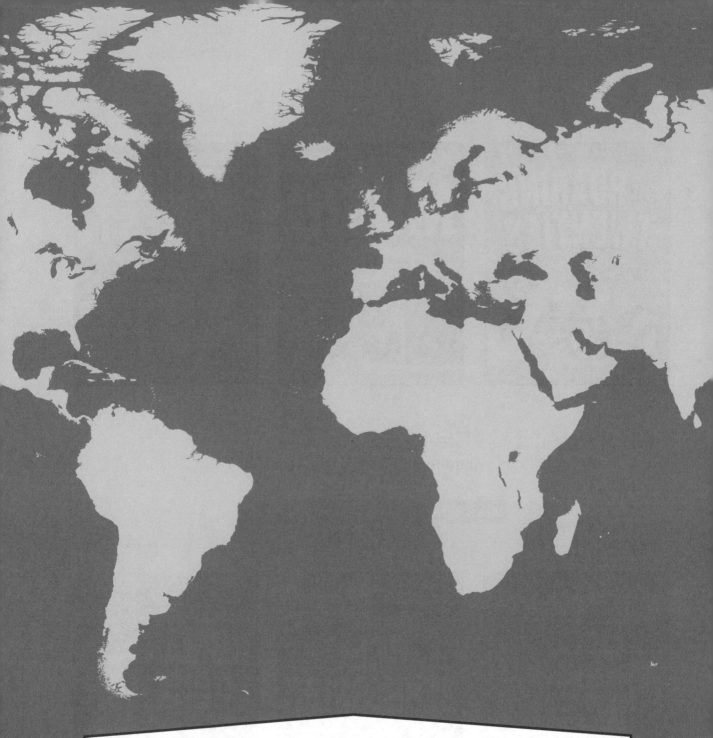

Interested in primary sources?

PS

Look for this icon.

You can use a smartphone or tablet app to scan the QR codes and explore more about human migration! Cover up neighboring QR codes to make sure you're scanning the right one. You can find a list of URLs on the Resources page.

If the QR code doesn't work, try searching the Internet with the Keyword Prompts to find other helpful sources. 🔍 human migration

Contents

Glossary ▾ **Resources** ▾ **Index**

TIMELINE

200,000 BCE............ *Homo sapiens* emerge in Africa as a distinct species. This is the species to which all living human beings on Earth belong.

74,000 BCE............... A super-volcano erupts on Mount Toba on the island of Sumatra. Tools found above and below the ash line left by this volcano help scientists develop theories about when the first humans traveled through Asia and what route they took.

70,000–60,000 BCE.... After coming close to extinction, the *Homo sapiens* population in Africa stabilizes and rebounds. Climate conditions affecting food and water availability prompt some humans to leave Africa and enter Asia for the first time.

55,000–50,000 BCE.... *Homo sapiens* migrate to Australia. During the last Ice Age, glaciers absorb so much sea water that humans can walk most of the way from Asia to Australia. However, they still have to navigate across 50 miles of open ocean.

52,000–45,000 BCE.... *Homo sapiens* migrate to Europe along a corridor of fertile land through the Middle East to southern Europe. There they encounter the last remaining human cousins—Neanderthal Man.

28,000 BCE............... Neanderthal is extinct. *Homo sapiens* is the only surviving human species.

16,500–13,500 BCE.... Humans migrate to the Americas. For decades, scientists believed the first humans could only have reached North America on foot over the land bridge from Asia. New scientific discoveries suggest some people might have traveled by boat and arrived much earlier than scientists previously believed possible.

3000–1000 BCE......... The Bantu-speaking people migrate across Africa. Scientists track their long, slow migration by analyzing linguistic patterns in modern languages that have their roots in Bantu.

132–1948 CE............ Religious intolerance repeatedly forces people of the Jewish faith out of their homelands. This scattering of the population is known as diaspora.

793–1150................ From their homeland in Scandinavia, Viking warriors launch raids on Western and Eastern Europe. They eventually establish trading posts and settlements in these lands.

1500–1850............... The transatlantic slave trade is the largest forced migration in history. At least 12 million people are captured from their homelands in Africa and shipped to Europe and the Americas, where they are sold into slavery. The Indian Ocean slave trade results in the capture and shipment of 3 to 5 million East Central Africans to the Middle East and South Asia.

During tens of thousands of years, humans have migrated around the earth to inhabit almost every continent. People continue to move from one place to another, bringing their ideas and cultures with them.

Fifty thousand years ago, a group of people stood at the edge of the lost continent of Sunda, in what is today south Asia. They faced a stretch of ocean at least 55 miles wide. On the distant shore lay New Guinea and Australia. In a feat of courage the world may have never seen before, these early humans built a crude raft, probably from bamboo, and launched themselves into the sea.

Fast forward to the spring of 2015. Three hundred men, women, and children huddle on the coast of Libya in North Africa. More than 1,000 miles of deceptively beautiful Mediterranean Sea separate them from what they seek—refuge in Europe. In an act of desperation the world sees often today, these families cram aboard a rickety wooden fishing boat and set sail.

Tens of thousands of years separate these two groups of people, but their stories have much in common. These people are migrating. They are people on the move from one place to another.

1607–1700............... The British colonize the east coast of North America. The 13 colonies that the British establish eventually become the United States of America.

1815–1915............... Millions of Europeans and thousands of Asians migrate to the United States in search of political freedom and economic opportunity.

1882–1943............... The Chinese Exclusion Act bars most Chinese from immigrating to the United States and bans all Chinese from becoming American citizens.

1910–1930............... Tens of thousands of African Americans move to northern states to escape racism and find better economic opportunities in a surge known as the Great Migration.

1933....................... Scientists discover a distinctive spearhead in Clovis, New Mexico. Similar tools found across the Americas are labeled as coming from the Clovis culture. For decades, scientists believe that the Clovis people were the first migrants into North America, but new evidence has cast doubt on that theory.

1942–1964............... As part of the Bracero Program, 4.5 million Mexican workers come to the United States as temporary farm laborers. They are poorly paid and forced to work in dangerous conditions.

1974....................... Scientist Jim Bowler discovers the remains of Mungo Man in a remote corner of Australia. These bones are 42,000 years old, which indicates that humans must have developed the technology to travel by water to Australia from Asia much earlier than scientists previously thought.

2004....................... Scientists discover the remains of a miniature human species on the Indonesian island of Flores. Known as *Homo floresiensis*, these skeletons share characteristics with ancient *Homo* species, but are dated to 18,000 years ago. Therefore, this primitive species existed on Earth at the same time as modern humans.

2008....................... The global financial crisis damages the Greek economy and tens of thousands of professional Greeks emigrate to find work.

2010....................... Scientists at the Max Planck Institute sequence the Neanderthal genome and discover that most people today share a small percentage of DNA with Neanderthal Man.

2011....................... The Syrian Civil War begins. More than 10 million Syrians are displaced by this violence.

2015....................... The United Nations reports that there are 60 million displaced people in the world.

Introductio

What Is Human Migration?

TIMELINE

1607–1700.............. The British colonize the east coast of North America. The 13 colonies that the British establish eventually become the United States of America.

1815–1915.............. Millions of Europeans and thousands of Asians migrate to the United States in search of political freedom and economic opportunity.

1882–1943.............. The Chinese Exclusion Act bars most Chinese from immigrating to the United States and bans all Chinese from becoming American citizens.

1910–1930.............. Tens of thousands of African Americans move to northern states to escape racism and find better economic opportunities in a surge known as the Great Migration.

1933..................... Scientists discover a distinctive spearhead in Clovis, New Mexico. Similar tools found across the Americas are labeled as coming from the Clovis culture. For decades, scientists believe that the Clovis people were the first migrants into North America, but new evidence has cast doubt on that theory.

1942–1964.............. As part of the Bracero Program, 4.5 million Mexican workers come to the United States as temporary farm laborers. They are poorly paid and forced to work in dangerous conditions.

1974..................... Scientist Jim Bowler discovers the remains of Mungo Man in a remote corner of Australia. These bones are 42,000 years old, which indicates that humans must have developed the technology to travel by water to Australia from Asia much earlier than scientists previously thought.

2004..................... Scientists discover the remains of a miniature human species on the Indonesian island of Flores. Known as *Homo floresiensis*, these skeletons share characteristics with ancient *Homo* species, but are dated to 18,000 years ago. Therefore, this primitive species existed on Earth at the same time as modern humans.

2008..................... The global financial crisis damages the Greek economy and tens of thousands of professional Greeks emigrate to find work.

2010..................... Scientists at the Max Planck Institute sequence the Neanderthal genome and discover that most people today share a small percentage of DNA with Neanderthal Man.

2011..................... The Syrian Civil War begins. More than 10 million Syrians are displaced by this violence.

2015..................... The United Nations reports that there are 60 million displaced people in the world.

What Is Human Migration?

How has human migration affected the world we live in today?

 **During tens of thousands of years, humans have migrated around the earth to inhabit almost every continent. People continue to move from one place to another, bringing their ideas and cultures with them.**

Fifty thousand years ago, a group of people stood at the edge of the lost continent of Sunda, in what is today south Asia. They faced a stretch of ocean at least 55 miles wide. On the distant shore lay New Guinea and Australia. In a feat of courage the world may have never seen before, these early humans built a crude raft, probably from bamboo, and launched themselves into the sea.

Fast forward to the spring of 2015. Three hundred men, women, and children huddle on the coast of Libya in North Africa. More than 1,000 miles of deceptively beautiful Mediterranean Sea separate them from what they seek—refuge in Europe. In an act of desperation the world sees often today, these families cram aboard a rickety wooden fishing boat and set sail.

Tens of thousands of years separate these two groups of people, but their stories have much in common. These people are migrating. They are people on the move from one place to another.